Little Honker's Backyard Adventures

Virginia K. White

Illustrated by
Gaspar Sabater

In Praise of Little Honker's Backyard Adventures

"A great book for animal lovers of all ages. It is educational as well as entertaining. Once you start reading, you can't put it down! Extremely enjoyable."
—*Margie Smith - Music Instructor, Denton, Nebraska*

"What a cute story! We have been fans of the Little Honker stories since the first book. I love that in this book, Warren's backyard is a place to hang out and socialize. I especially liked that Warren's role as a leader has changed a bit. What will Fanta do next?"
—*Kristin K. Dulany - Nurse, Wellington, Colorado*

"Warren's experiences are very much like some a child has in real life. Readers will readily engage in and relate to this book with the author's ability to combine fiction and nonfiction throughout the entire story."
—*Shirley Foster Key - Educator, Omaha, Nebraska*

"I love the book for its story and encouragement to want to read further. I also like the teaching moments when child and adult are reading together."
—Doris Gierhan - Educator, Ligonier, Indiana

"This book has so many research and discussion topics to expand upon. From learning about the characteristics of various animals to how to be a good neighbor, this book is filled with fantastic food for thought. I especially liked the message of parental concern for where children are and the need to be cautious."
—Marinell Neuhaus - Educator, Omaha, Nebraska

"Warren's latest adventure with the newest residents and neighbors of his backyard will resonate with anyone still searching for his or her "tribe." Finding the people that you share things with is a challenge, but Warren takes that challenge and makes it look easy. You don't have to be just like your friends, but if you have one thing in common with each other, you have the seed to make a friendship grow. Find that one thing!"
—Staci Day - Elementary School Educator

"I've always loved Virginia's books and that is because I can totally relate to her clear intention of teaching us, the readers, valuable lessons. Through Little Honker we get to live amazing adventures, we face the unknown, and we even find ourselves in difficult situations sometimes. But our favorite little Siamese cat always shows us the way, and also that, with the help of your friends and loved ones, you can achieve all your dreams."

—*Gaspar Sabater - Professional Illustrator and Cartoonist*

Little Honker's Backyard Adventures
© 2018 Virginia K. White

All Rights Reserved. No part of this book may be reproduced or transmitted in any form or by any means, electronic or mechanical, including photocopying, recording, or by any information storage and retrieval system, without permission in writing from the publisher.

This book is a work of fiction. Characters, names, places, and incidents are fictitious or used fictitiously. Any similarity to real persons, living or dead, or events, is coincidental and not intended by the author.

Illustrated by Gaspar Sabater

Cover Design by AM Design Studios

Distributed by Bublish, Inc.
bublish.com

ISBN: 9780999062869

Also by Virginia K. White

Little Honker Saves the Day

Little Honker's Winter Concert

Little Honker and the Swinging Tails

Glasses for Margie

(coming soon)
The Swinging Tails Hit the Stage

Would You Like A Scarlet Striped Schrinkler?

To

All two legged and four legged creatures who search for adventures and friendships in their own way. Let the magic come through!

Can a cat have magical powers? Are cats able to predict a future event? From Egyptian times to the present, cats in many cultures are considered both lucky and magical. Is Little Honker one of those magical cats?

Table of Contents

1. Spring Life in the Backyard ... 1
2. The Escape ... 7
3. Oops ... 11
4. Dreamland Adventure ... 16
5. Dreamland's Help and More ... 20
6. Wake-up Call ... 26
7. A New Routine ... 30
8. Sold! ... 34
9. Help Arrives ... 37
10. Magical Powers ... 46
11. Backyard Surprise ... 50

Chapter One
Spring Life in the Backyard

Warren was a honker. His feline family were meowers. Warren tried and tried to meow like his family, but he couldn't. Honking was his meow. He got used to it. His feline family got used to it. His human family got used to it. So, he became Little Honker and he got used to it.

Warren loved spring. He loved to sit on the windowsill and watch spring come to life in his backyard. He remembered, when he was a kitten, how much he enjoyed chasing butterflies and climbing trees in search of birds. He enjoyed smelling all of the blooming flowers, pulling the stems back, and then watching them bounce into place again. He was older now and wanted more adventures. How would he be able to do that?

With spring came new life and new adventures.

New adventures intrigued him. Warren eagerly sought them out. He wanted to escape the inside of the house and do some backyard exploring on his own. No brothers or sisters. No mom or dad. No humans. But, when would he get the chance?

Today, as he looked out the window, he noticed two new visitors. They did not look like anything he had seen before in his backyard. He honked and honked. The visitors were picking things out of the ground to eat. He honked again. "Who were these strangers? Were these strangers looking for a new adventure too?" he wondered.

Warren's honk brought his mother, Bernice, and his two human girls, Kari and Kris, to his side. "Who are these visitors?" Warren honked.

Before Bernice could respond, the girls said "Oh my gosh! We have two mallard ducks in our backyard."

"Where did they come from?" Kari asked.

"I have no idea," Kris said. "We have never had ducks in our backyard. I think maybe the pond Dad put in attracted them," she continued.

For a few minutes, Bernice, Warren, Kari, and Kris watched the duck activity. Not only were the ducks searching for food, but it seemed like the female was also gathering dead grass and leaves.

Little Honker's Backyard Adventure

Kari said, "Look Kris, I think the female is making a nest in the planter Dad placed under the bushes."

"You're right," Kris said. "If the female is making a nest here, she must feel safe."

"Looks like they will be here for a while," Kari said. "Let's name them."

Kari was always eager to find names for animals, even visiting ones.

"How about Morgan and Mildred?" Kris suggested.

"I like it," Kari said. "Morgan and Mildred it is!"

With that, the girls left, but Warren and Bernice stayed to watch a bit longer. The open window let the cool spring breeze in and Warren heard Mildred make a sound similar to his. Morgan responded in a slightly different way, but it was also similar to Warren's honk.

"They sound like me," he honked to Bernice.

"Yes, they do sound a bit like you," Bernice meowed.

"I want to go talk to them," Warren honked.

Not so fast," Bernice warned. "You might scare them. Just watch and let them feel safe. They seem to be making a home here." Bernice rubbed Warren's head with hers, jumped down from the windowsill, and curled up in her basket.

Day after day Warren perched upon the windowsill to observe the visitors. He watched them gather items for the nest, look for food, and swim around in the pond. His tail went back and forth and from time to time, he honked out the window. He really wanted to talk to those ducks. After several days of observing and giving an occasional honk out the window, he decided it was time to get outside and talk to the new visitors.

He thought he had waited long enough for them to get settled, so when the perfect opportunity arrived, he planned to slip right out of the door so he could talk to them.

And then it happened!

Chapter Two

The Escape

The opportunity door opened as Kari went out to fill the bird feeder. She did not notice that Warren slipped out right behind her when she opened the door.

Morgan and Mildred were moving around in the water. Warren thought if he quietly went over to the edge of the pond, he would be able to talk to them. She was unaware of his escape as she left the house and walked over to the birdfeeder. He felt safe and quietly approached the edge of the pond and honked softly. No need to bring his escape to Kari's attention.

Both ducks turned and looked at him. He didn't look like them, but he sounded similar to them.

Warren honked, "Hello. Welcome to my backyard. What are you doing here? Do you like the water?"

Mildred honked back, "It's wonderful. Come on in. Why do you sound like us but look so different? What is your name?"

"My name is Warren, but my family sometimes calls me Little Honker. I have never been able to meow like my family. It's OK. I'm a Seal Point Siamese cat who looks and sounds different than my family. But, I've found honking can be very useful. Last spring I saved my family from an unwanted visitor in the yard, and I discovered that I love music. I help my girls practice the piano and saxophone. I even played the bells at a winter concert. I heard you are mallard ducks."

Morgan swam over to Warren and honked, "We are, indeed, mallard ducks. Come on in the water. It feels great."

"I've never been IN the water. I drink water out of a bowl. I'm not sure I'd like to get all wet. My feet are not like yours and my tail is different," Warren honked.

Carefully Warren put his paw in the water. He pulled it out, shook it, and then licked it. "I'm not sure I like this water," he honked. What do you call what you are doing?"

"It's called swimming," Mildred said. "We swim differently than some animals, but we love the water and moving about in our own way."

"When we saw this pond and the perfect place under the bushes, we decided we wanted to make a home here," Morgan said.

"It's the perfect place to raise our family," Mildred said.

"I wondered why you were taking leaves and grass over to that planter. This is a great place to live. I hope you like it here," Warren continued.

"Do come in for a swim. The water is perfect this morning, Morgan said.

"We'd love to have you join us. Just take the plunge," Mildred said encouragingly.

Even though Warren didn't immediately like the idea of getting in the water, he was always ready for something new. He reasoned that just because they sounded like him but looked different should not prevent him from joining them. They did, after all, invite him in for a swim. They seemed to enjoy it, so why not?

Warren plunged!

Chapter Three

Oops

Splash! Warren was in the pond trying to swim like Morgan and Mildred. He was working his legs as fast as he could. But, he could not swim like his duck friends. In fact, he could not swim at all! Still, he was giving it a try. He was paddling as fast as he could, but he was having trouble keeping his head above water. This swimming thing was much more difficult than he thought it would be.

And then it happened. Warren started to go under. He was paddling as fast as he could but kept sinking. With every bob of his head out of the water, he was honking for help. "Honk. Honk," he said in his loudest Siamese cat voice. His head continued to bob in and out of the water and his legs were moving in every direction trying to get to the edge of the pond. He was gasping for air. "Honk. Honk. Where is Kari now that I need her," he asked himself.

Morgan and Mildred were in the pond giving him instructions.

"Just keep paddling," Morgan said.

"Work your front legs more," Mildred suggested.

"I. . .am. . .," Warren honked. "I. . .am. . .sinking."

"Just work your legs back and forth more. That always works for me," said Morgan.

"I. . . (gasp) . . .am. . .(gasp) not. . .(gasp) . . . like (gasp). . .you," Warren honked.

Suddenly there was another splash in the pond. Warren felt a push, a shove, and the next thing he knew, he was at the edge of the pond. He pulled himself up, shook himself off, and looked around.

He saw another cat. Big, mostly black, and soaking wet just like he was.

"Who are you? Where did you come from?" Warren asked.

"I jumped over the fence when I heard your honks. You're a cat. Why do you honk?" the new arrival asked.

"My honk is my meow. I was born this way," Warren said. "What's your name? Where do you live?"

"I go by Fanta. We are moving in next to you."

"You seem to like the water. Even though I like new adventures, I don't think the water is a good adventure for me. As you saw, swimming is something I can not do very well," Warren said.

"I know cats aren't supposed to like the water, but I love it! I always get in the shower after my people get out. I love to get in sinks when I can. I love running water! And, one time I even jumped in the bath water when Kaycee, one of my humans, was taking a bath. The disappointing thing was that it was a bubble bath! I can't say I was very fond of the bubbles," Fanta said.

"Well, thanks for your help," Warren honked. "Welcome to my backyard. I liked talking to my new feathered friends, but I don't think they could understand that I was not able to swim quite like them."

"Hey, what's your name?" Fanta asked.

"My name is Warren, but sometimes my family calls me Little Honker. I've always been smaller than my brothers and sisters and I don't sound like them. Honking is my meow."

"I like it. I'm calling you Honker," Fanta said. "Think I'll join your feathered friends for a swim and then soak up some sun."

Off Fanta went to the pond. "Do you mind if I join you?" she asked Morgan and Mildred.

"Come in. The water is great," Morgan said.

"Do join us," said Mildred. "You seem to like swimming better than Warren."

"I love it!" With that, Fanta took the plunge, made a big splash, and swam around with her new friends.

Warren looked on in amazement. "How does she

do that?" he asked himself. "I wish I could be in the water with them, but I keep sinking. Maybe Fanta can give me some lessons."

Warren jumped up on a lawn chair which was in a sunny spot and curled up for a nap. Warm sun invited a great nap.

Warren gave a kitty smile and started to think about his new backyard friends. They were different than he was, but he really liked talking to them. As he entered Dreamland, he started to think about the home his new friends were making and the pond. The nest Mildred was making would mean babies soon. "I wonder what the babies will be like? I wonder what else Fanta likes besides swimming?" he asked himself as he closed his eyes and fell asleep. Dreamland meant more adventures.

Chapter Four
Dreamland Adventure

"Warren, will you watch the babies for me?" Mildred asked. "I'm off to find some food for them."

Warren paddled over to the edge of the pond in his floater. "Send them in." With his floater on, Little Honker felt very confident.

The ducklings jumped into the pond and immediately swam over to Warren.

"Want to play?" one of them asked. "I love to dive down into the water. Want to do that?"

"Hey, why are you in that thing? What is it?" another duckling asked.

"Well, I'm not very good at swimming. If I have this floater on, then I can paddle around almost as well as you can."

"Hey. You sound like us, but you don't look anything like us," another duckling said.

"You don't have feathers. What do they call that stuff that is all over you?"

"I'm a Siamese cat and I have fur not feathers. My tail also looks different than yours," Warren said.

"Where is it? I can't see a tail."

"It's under the water with the rest of my body. I only have part of my body out of the water because I'm holding on to the floater," Warren explained.

"I'm diving down to see the rest of you," a duckling said and made a dive close to Warren.

In no time the duckling popped up and said, "I saw your tail and the rest of you. You sure look different than we do. But, you sound kind of like us."

"I do sound similar to you. I'm a cat, but I can't meow like other cats. I honk. It's OK. I found that honking can be a good thing. Swimming is a good thing for you. Swimming does not seem to be a good thing for me."

"We love it! It's so much fun to paddle around in

the water and make dives down deep into the water."

"Can we hang on and float with you? It looks like fun."

"OK with me," Warren honked.

All four of the ducklings jumped onto the floater and rode around the pond as Warren paddled from one end to the other.

"This is great!" one of the babies honked. "I think I can make a good dive from this thing." And off he went.

His siblings soon followed and then popped up out of the water.

"Dive with us, Warren. You'll love it." All four ducklings said.

Little Honker's Backyard Adventure

Even though Warren was not a good swimmer, he still wanted to give it a try. New adventures were always something he was eager to try. He ducked under the floater and thought he could dive like the babies. He did give it a try, but it did not work well. What was he thinking? He was in the floater because he could not swim like the ducks. He was gasping for air and paddling as fast as he could. Was he going to sink to the bottom of the pond? What was he going to do? He was supposed to be taking care of the babies and he was

...sinking

...sinking

...sinking.

He started to honk as he gasped for air. He needed help! He honked and honked and honked.

Chapter Five
Dreamland's Help and More

"Help me!" he honked as loudly as he could while gasping for air.

The ducklings started firing questions in Warren's direction.

"What's wrong, Warren?"

"Why can't you get back in your floater?"

"Can't you just swim to the edge and get out?"

And then one of the ducklings said, "You really are not very good at this swimming thing."

"Help me!" Warren honked again. "I can't (gasp) swim (gasp)." Warren was moving in the direction of the edge, but he kept going under the water. Every time his head popped out of the water, he gasped for air.

All four ducklings came paddling as fast as their little legs would let them. Instinct set in and the ducklings went into action.

"Hold on, Warren. We'll help you swim to the side so you can get out."

Warren had two front paws on two ducklings and they were all swimming to the side of the pond. Warren was working his hind feet as fast as he could and holding on to the sides of two of the ducklings. The two in the back were pushing Warren and trying desperately to keep him afloat. When they got there, he put his front paws on the edge of the pond and two of the babies pushed and pushed and pushed him with their heads from the back.

They pushed and pushed until finally his back side was out of the water. Those ducklings had way more superpower than Warren could ever imagine.

"Wow! Your tail is long and it doesn't look anything like ours."

"No wonder you can't swim very well."

"Thanks guys! You saved me. I think I'll just watch you from the side of the pond. You are better swimmers than I am.

"I need some sun and a nap. I'll talk to you later." As Warren left the pond, he noticed Fanta had returned. There were two other cats with her.

Warren honked. "Fanta, you are back. Who are your friends?"

Fanta stood up, stretched, and said, "This is my mom, Sprite, and my step-dad, Willy. I told them about your great backyard and they wanted to come see for themselves. We all jumped over, but jumping is not a favorite of Mom or Willy."

All three cats were resting on lawn chairs. Willy, a beautiful tuxedo cat with a stub tail, seemed pretty quiet. He was close to Sprite, a gorgeous tortoise shell cat with a little yellow mustache.

"When did you come over? I didn't see you," Warren said.

"You were in the pond trying to swim with the ducklings. I must say, you were not doing a very good job," Fanta said.

"What did you all do when you came over? I didn't even notice you were here," Warren said.

"No wonder you didn't see us. You were having quite a time in the water, but the ducklings seemed to have things under control, so I didn't jump in to help," Fanta continued. "We just explored your yard.

Chased some butterflies, climbed a few trees, looked for some birds, and talked to Morgan and Mildred who were gathering food."

"Hey, why do you honk?" Willy asked as he stood up and stretched his full 24 inches in length.

"I was born this way. I tried to meow like my family, but honking seems to be my meow. We all got used to it. Some people call me Little Honker," Warren responded.

Then Warren noticed Willy's tail. It was a stub of a tail, not the usual cat tail. "Hey, what happened to your tail?" Warren asked.

"None of your business!" Willy hissed. He started to puff his fur and was ready to jump on Little Honker when Sprite reached over and placed a paw on his head.

"Willy and I are rescue cats. He doesn't talk about his life before they found him. He was pretty sick and it took a long time before he became healthy. Lots of vet visits and special food. We met at FUR the Love of Paws FURcility. I was pregnant. He has always been protective of us, but you never talk about his past. I think it must have been pretty bad. He just wants to forget it."

"I got it. What's a recue cat? What is a FURcility?" Warren asked.

"The FUR the Love of Paws FURcility is a place for animals to stay and get healthy until they can find a forever home," Sprite explained.

"I've never heard of that. I've always lived here with my family," Warren said.

"You're lucky. But, we are lucky too. The caregivers named me Sprite and I had six babies that they named after sodas. Willy has always been protective of us," Sprite said. "All of the caregivers at the FURcility took amazing care of all of us."

"That's great. What happened to your other babies?" Warren asked.

"They all found forever homes and are very happy. RC and Squirt were adopted together by a great family who needed them. I'm so happy for them. Fresca and Shasta also found a forever home together with a loving family. Surge was adopted separately because the family adopted another cat from the FURcility the year before. We were excited when the three of us were adopted together. We became a family in the FURcility and a very nice couple decided we should stay together and brought us all to live with them next to you," Sprite said. "We were lucky again."

"Welcome to our neighborhood," Warren said.

"Thanks," Sprite said. "Looks like you are ready for a nap after your swimming adventure."

"I think you're right," Warren said. "That adventure wore me out!"

"Take a good nap. That always helps me," Fanta said. "Mom, Willy, we should let Honker nap."

"You're right," Sprite said. "Willy, let's see what is going on in our own backyard."

"See you later, Honker," Willy said.

With that, all three cats jumped over the fence and Warren curled up on the lawn chair to nap.

Chapter Six
Wake-up Call

The sun was fading and it had started to cool off. Warren opened his blue eyes and realized he was still outside. His fur was dry, but it was not as smooth as usual. He began giving himself a bath and then decided he needed a little bit of human assistance. His fur was matted. He didn't like it. It felt strange. He could not smooth it out. He needed help from his girls. So, he jumped from the chair, headed for the back door, and started to honk.

Kari came to the door and looked at Warren's matted fur. "What in the world happened to you Warren? And, why are you outside?" She opened the door to let in their matted fur ball kitty and said, "Kris, come here. Warren has managed to get himself in a bit of a mess.

Little Honker's Backyard Adventure

"Warren, how did your fur get into such a mess?" Kris asked.

"I was swimming with my new friends in the pond," Warren honked.

"Cats can't really swim that well," Kari said. "What were you thinking?"

"They were having so much fun in the pond and invited me to join them, so I jumped in and gave it a try. It did not work out well. They are much better than I am at swimming."

"They are made to be swimmers, Warren. It is true that you can do many unusual things for a cat, but it looks like swimming is not one of them," Kris said.

"That's true. But, I really liked talking to them. And, the babies helped me get out of the pond when

I was having trouble."

"What? There are no babies out there yet," the girls both said at once.

Warren smiled and gave each of them a kitty kiss.

"Warren, why don't you come over here so we can brush you out," Kris said.

"You never let your fur get into this kind of a mess," Kari said as she started to brush out the matted fur.

"Do you think you learned your lesson?" Kris asked.

"And, I met three new cats who are moving in next door. Fanta, Sprite, and Willy. They are rescue cats and lived in a FURcility until they were adopted by the people who are moving in next door. Fanta loves the water and can really swim! Willy only has part of his tail and you don't ask him about it. He gets upset. And, Sprite is Fanta's mom. She had six kittens in the FURcility and they all found forever homes."

"The house next to us is still for sale, Honker. There is not a family living there yet and there are no cats," Kari said.

"You have quite an imagination, Warren. We love your creativity, but this story is a bit unusual even for you," Kris said.

Warren just purred as the girls groomed him.

When they were finished, he gave them a kitty kiss and walked over to his basket. It was time to curl up, nap, and reflect upon his day. As he nestled in, he thought about tomorrow and how much fun he would have outside with his new found friends. He decided he would not swim again. That was one adventure he was not fond of repeating. But, something new might be waiting for him to try. He could hardly wait to see what it would be. Curled up in his basket, feeling warm, smoothed out, and comfortable, he was ready for a good nap.

Chapter Seven
A New Routine

As the days passed, Little Honker thought more and more about his outside adventure. He really wanted to expand his outside routine. After his big escape, he wanted more time in the backyard and more time to talk to his new friends. But, he still did not want to swim. After waiting several days, it was time for THE talk.

"I really like my new feathered friends," Warren said to Kari and Kris. "I'd like to go visit them more often. Sorry I escaped and you didn't know where I was."

"It sure was a surprise," Kari said. "Usually you just go out in back with the rest of your family and that isn't very often."

"I know. But, I could hardly wait to find out more about those ducks! They sounded like me but didn't look like me. I wanted to know more," Warren honked.

"I know. You are curious for sure," Kris said. "You need to be careful so you don't get yourself into another mess."

"No more swimming, but I do like to talk to them," Warren said. "Mildred and Morgan are starting to take turns sitting on the eggs."

"I didn't even notice that," Kari said.

"When did you see that, Honker?" Kris asked.

"I've been watching them for a while out of the kitchen window. They really seem to care for each other," Warren said.

"I think mallard ducks mate for life," Kari said.

"That's right. So, it is natural that they would care of each other," Kris said.

"What good parents they will be for their ducklings," Kari said. "It will be so much fun when there are babies in the yard and swimming in the pond!"

"So, do you think I could start going outside more often to talk to them?" Warren pleaded.

"I think it would be fine as long as you don't try the swimming thing again," Kris said. "You were a mess."

"And, we don't want anything to happen to you," Kari said. "You are our special Little Honker who practices with us and sends all of us on new adventures."

"OK. Can I go talk to them now?" Warren asked.

"Just don't get into any more messes little guy," Kris said.

"It took us quite a while to get your fur smoothed out," Kari said.

On that note, Little Honker went to the patio door, gave a soft honk asking for the door to be opened, and waited patiently for one of his girls to open the door.

Little Honker's Backyard Adventure

"Some patio doors have little doors for pets to go in and out all by themselves," Warren said.

"They do," Kris said. "But, I'm not so sure that would be a good idea at this house." Who knows what might be coming inside to visit us.

"I think we will leave it at "Permission Only" for now," Kari said. "Just let us know when you want to go outside."

"OK," Warren said. "I'll honk when I want to come in."

"Or, we might come to the door and call you. We would hate to have you miss dinner," Kris said.

Kris opened the door and Little Honker went outside to honk with Morgan and Mildred.

"Have fun, Warren," Kari said. "We'll let you know when it is time to come inside."

"And, no swimming little buddy," Kris said.

"No way will I decide to take another plunge," Warren honked as he walked to the pond. "See you later."

Chapter Eight
Sold!

Minutes later Kris looked out the front window and said, "Kari, come quick. There's a moving van next door. It looks like the house next door to us sold and the family is moving in."

"That's so cool!" Kari said. "I wonder if they have any kids or pets."

"Let's go introduce ourselves after they get settled a bit," Kris said.

"We have lots of changes around here. First Morgan and Mildred moved in and now we have a new family next door," Kari said. "Never a dull moment around here. I like it. More adventures."

"You sound like Honker. He's always looking for something new," Kris said. "It's kind of exciting though."

"I think Mildred's eggs have hatched," Kari said. "I'm sure I saw the ducklings waddling around the nest."

"Really?" asked Kris. "Wonder when that happened."

"Well, Morgan and Mildred made the nest about a month ago," Kari said. "Seems about right. We don't go out in the back that often, so we probably missed all the nest sitting and gathering of food."

"Honker knew. Do you remember he mentioned that? He's been watching out the kitchen window a lot lately," Kris said.

"Do you remember those crazy stories he told us about the ducklings saving him and the family with cats who moved in next door?" Kris asked as she continued.

"Sure do. He does have a big imagination," Kari said.

"And, lots of creativity! He always keeps us on

our toes with his ideas."

"You got that right!" Kris said. "I don't think we've ever had a cat like the Little Honker."

"So true. But, he's a keeper for sure!" Kari said. Kari looked out the front window and noticed three kids carrying boxes into the house next door. "Hey, our new neighbors have kids. It looks like two girls and a boy."

"Do you think it would be rude to go meet them this soon?" Kris asked.

"Let's do it! We can offer to carry in some boxes and then we would have a chance to talk to them," Kari said.

"OK. Let's go introduce ourselves," Kris said.

In a flash, the girls were headed to the door when Kari remembered that Little Honker was outside. She went to the patio door; Honker was talking to Morgan and Mildred. "We're going to meet our new neighbors, Honker. Stay out of the water."

Little Honker turned and said, "Tell Fanta, Sprite, and Willy I said honk. I wanted you to meet them."

"What are you talking about?" Kari asked. She turned to Kris and said, "I think our Little Honker is imagining things. He just told me to say hello to Fanta, Sprite, and Willy."

"Who are they?" Kris asked.

"I have no idea. Let's go meet our new neighbors," Kari said.

Chapter Nine
Help Arrives

Kari and Kris walked next door to meet their new neighbors. The entire family was unloading the moving van and carrying furniture and boxes into the house. The parents were handling the larger items and the kids were handling various smaller items. It was team work at its best for a challenging job.

"Can we help you with something?" Kari asked. "We live next door and thought you might need some help. My name is Kari and this is my sister Kris."

"Thanks. I think we could use some help. Moving is not much fun, but our new house is pretty cool. I'm Sheridan and this is my brother Garrett and my sister Kaycee."

"Glad to meet you," Kris said. "Welcome to the neighborhood."

"Thanks. I think we are going to like it here," Sheridan said as she picked up a box. "If you really want to help, Kris, you could carry the box that's marked 'dishes.'"

"Sounds good," Kris said.

Kari climbed into the moving van and asked Garrett if she could carry in the box next to her. Garrett had a good sized box ready to take into the house and he said, "That would be great. Seems like we have more boxes for the kitchen than almost anything else."

"It takes lots of pots and pans plus all the things you need when you start to cook and set up a kitchen," Kay said. "Hi. My name is Kay and this is my husband Gayle. Thanks for coming over to help us out."

"Glad to help. We remember how much work moving can be! We love this neighborhood and we hope you do too," Kari said.

"We heard this town was a good place to raise a family. So far everyone has been extremely helpful," Kay said. "Your help reassured us that we made a good choice."

"Plus, we love the fact that there is an animal clinic so close to us," Gayle said. "With three new rescue cats, we thought that would be a great idea."

"That clinic belongs to our dad," Kari said proudly.

"We love being close to the clinic too because we have cats and we get to see all kinds of interesting animals," Kris said.

"Wow! That is super cool!" Garrett said. "I bet your dad sees all kinds of dogs, cats, and maybe even some exotic animals."

"He does for sure. Lots of fun and fascinating stories around our dinner table," Kari said. "We have received a good animal education."

"I would love to hear more of the stories, but I think we need to get things out of the van and into the house before my energy is gone," Gayle said. "I'm taking the last of the kitchen stuff in. Talk to you all later. Thanks for the help."

"Moving always makes a person think about what has been saved and what is going to work in the new place," Kay commented. "We donated so many things before we moved. How do we still have this much to move in?"

"I know what you mean," Kari said. "We donated lots of stuff too before we moved here, but it seems like we are filling up this house again."

"We found that some of the things we thought would work in the new house, really didn't work as we thought they would," Kris said.

"I'm afraid we are discovering a bit of that now," Kay said.

"Let's see what else is left in the van and we can help move those things into the house," Kari said.

Kaycee hopped into the van to help when Kari noticed something she had never seen before. "What is this?" she asked Kaycee as she looked at an enormous wheel propped up to the side of the van. "I've never seen anything like it."

"That's an exercise wheel for my cat Fanta. It's kind of like a treadmill. Fanta gets on that thing and goes and goes. She loves it and it builds up her leg muscles," Kaycee explained. "She has pretty strong legs because she loves to get on it and run. It isn't heavy. It's just big."

Kaycee turned to Garrett and said, "I'm going to carry the base in Garrett."

"Sounds good. I'll get the wheel," Garrett said.

"You have a cat named Fanta? " Kris asked. She looked at Kari and said, "Didn't Honker say something about a cat named Fanta?"

"Yes he did," Kris said. "Just a coincidence I guess."

"We do have a cat named Fanta," Kaycee said. "We actually have three cats. Sprite is Fanta's mom and we have Willy too. We adopted them from a rescue place."

"OK this is pretty strange," Kari said to Kris. "I am sure Honker said something about Sprite and Willy. What is going on here?"

"I know. This *is* very strange," Kris said. "You never know about that Little Honker. I think we will have a chat when we go home."

Suddenly Garrett was on the scene and said, "They all became a family in the FURcility and none of us wanted to separate them. Sprite had babies in the rescue place and Willy came in later."

"We heard that Willy was really sick when they found him and most of his tail had been cut off," Sheridan said. "Nobody knows how it happened, but he loves his girls so much that we couldn't stand to separate them."

"And Willy?" Kris said as she turned to Kari. "Definitely time to talk to Honker.

"Has Honker met our cats?" Garrett asked. "You are talking like he has."

"I don't think so, but he does have quite an imagination," Kris said.

That's such a great story about your cats," Kari said. "Where are they? I don't think we have seen them since we have been moving things into the house."

"We let them explore in the backyard for a bit. They seem to enjoy the trees and looking around," Sheridan said.

Little Honker's Backyard Adventure

"Aren't you afraid they will escape?" Kris asked.

"They're really good about staying together and the fence is pretty high, so I don't think they will jump over," Garrett said.

"We have cats too," Kari said. "Bernice and Bernard were our first cats and then they had five kittens. Warren, our little honker, is really the only one who wants to go outside very much."

"Wow, that is so awesome that you have so many cats," Kaycee said. "Why do you say Warren is a little honker?"

"Well, he doesn't have the usual meow," Kris explained. "He honks instead of meowing. We're all used to it and it's actually become pretty useful. He warned his family of a skunk in the backyard one time and he's pretty musical."

Kari said. "He's actually a fun guy and is always eager for new adventures."

"We should have our cats meet sometime," Kaycee said. "It might be lots of fun."

"Great idea," Kris said. "Maybe we can set something up later after you guys are a little more settled."

"That's an awesome idea," Garrett said. "I'm going to bring in the wheel and put it in the basement. I think we are close to cleaning out the van. The fun starts now!"

"Unpacking is just as much fun as packing," Sheridan said. "I hope I remember where I put stuff."

"I marked all of my stuff," Garrett said. "And, I have it in my room already."

"Show off," Kaycee said. "Most of mine is marked, but I don't have it in my room yet."

"We can help you with that, Kaycee," Kari said. "Kris, let's give this girl a hand."

"I'm on it!" Kris said. "Which room is yours, Kaycee?"

"Down the hall and to the right," Kaycee responded.

"Sheridan, do you need some help with your boxes?" Kari asked.

"I only have a few left. I think I can manage it. I'm not eager to unload it all though," Sheridan said.

"I know what you mean," Kris said. "It's another mess and a bit of a mystery to be solved."

"The challenge will soon begin," Sheridan said.

"Good luck, Sheridan, " Kari said. "You'll be so glad when everything is in its place."

"I know it," Sheridan said. "Thanks for all of the help."

"No problem," Kris said. "It was fun to meet all of you. Let us know if you need anything else."

Kris turned to Kari and said, "I think maybe we better check on Honker."

"Right. He's probably talking to the ducks again. But, no swimming for him," Kris said.

"Do you have a pool?" Garrett asked.

"No, just the pond Dad put in. We have some mallards who have made a nest in the back and Warren likes to talk to them. All honkers you know," Kari said.

"Great meeting you guys," Kris said. "Let's try to get our cats together soon."

"Have fun getting organized," Kari said.

All three kids said, "Thanks for the help."

Chapter Ten
Magical Powers

Kari and Kris walked home thinking about Fanta, Sprite, and Willy. Was it just a coincidence that the cats next door had names that Honker mentioned before they left the house, or did he have some kind of special powers. He was, indeed, an unusual cat and could do many things other cats could not do, but this was the most unusual thing he had ever done.

"Kris, do you remember when we studied Egypt in Mr. Muldoon's World History class?" Kari asked. "I think he told us that the Egyptian cats were believed to be magical creatures, capable of bringing luck to people who housed them."

"I do remember that. They had a spiritual importance, were sacred, and I also remember the part about magical powers," Kris said.

"Do you think Little Honker has some kind of

magical powers? I mean how did he know there would be cats moving in next door with the names Fanta, Sprite, and Willy?" Kari asked. "It seems like he can sense some future things."

"I know. He also told us about Fanta moving in next door when we didn't even know the house had been sold," Kris said. "This is just too weird!"

"I think we need to see if we can clear some of this up. We always knew he wasn't the typical cat, but this is so far out there that even I can't believe it," Kari said.

When the girls entered the house, they decided they would have a chat with their special Little Honker to see if they could find out how he knew about the new neighbors who had rescue cats. They found him sitting by the patio door waiting to come inside. He had finished his nap, talked to Morgan and Mildred, and he was ready to come inside for a snack.

"Hey Little Honker," Kari said. "We just met our new neighbors and heard about Fanta, Sprite, and Willy."

"How did you know about that before we did?" Kris asked.

"Well, Fanta came over the fence and saved me from sinking and then I had a dream about all of the cats," Warren said. "It just came to me when I was napping on the lawn chair."

"Fanta actually came over the fence and into our yard?" asked Kari.

"Yes, she really likes water and her legs are strong," Warren said.

"Kari turned to Kris and said, "Do you remember that Kaycee said Fanta loved that wheel and she ran and ran on it?"

"I do," Kris said. "I also remember Kaycee saying that her legs were strong. I guess she probably did have the strength to jump over the fence."

"I don't think our new neighbors know that, however. Remember that they said the cats were in the backyard and that they didn't think they could get over the fence," Kari said.

"Right. Guess they were wrong about Fanta," Kris said. "I'm glad she helped you out of the water, Warren."

"She loves the water and swimming with Morgan and Mildred," Honker said.

Warren went over to his food dish, had a bit of a snack, and then turned to his girls. "Maybe all of Fanta's family can come over soon. It would be fun.

Can I go out to tell Morgan and Mildred?" Honker asked

"OK. Just don't take another plunge. Fanta might not be there to save you," Kari said.

Kari open the patio door and Warren was out the door and over to the pond in no time.

Chapter Eleven
Backyard Surprise

With the "Permission Only" plan in place, Little Honker continued to visit the backyard as often as permission was granted. The ducklings were waddling around the yard now and swimming in the pond. Kari and Kris's dad added some fish to the pond and the ducklings dove down, swam with the new additions, and then popped back to the surface.

Fanta, Sprite, and Willy decided Warren's backyard was a fun playground and came visiting often. Up, over, and down. Fanta was in the yard and ready for play. Honker was on the edge of the pond talking to the ducklings.

"Hey Honker, mind if I go for a swim?" Fanta asked.

"Go for it. I think the ducklings are getting used

to you swimming with them," he said.

With that, Fanta plunged into the water and swam around with the four ducklings. Morgan and Mildred were resting under the Lilac bush but keeping a close eye on the pond activity. By now they had become used to Fanta's daily swim routine and knew she just loved the water and would not harm their babies.

"Hi Honker. Mind if we join you?" Sprite asked as she entered the backyard.

"You're all welcome to come over and play or rest," Warren said. "I know you both prefer not to jump the fence. Who brought you over today?"

"Sheridan, Garrett, and Kaycee," Sprite said. "Kari and Kris asked if they wanted to watch a movie."

Willy, as usual, stayed close to Sprite, while she talked to Honker. Fanta was still enjoying the water.

Suddenly there was an additional visitor. All backyard occupants saw it. Heads perked up, all facing the direction of the new visitor. It was long and looked similar to Honker in coloring, but walked close to the ground.

"Who is this visitor?" asked Warren.

Willy perked up and took a long look at the newcomer. "I've seen something like this," he said. He stood on all fours now and moved closer to the newcomer. He was at least twice the size of this visitor and three times the weight. Would there be an attack?

Sprite was frozen in place. Fanta jumped out of the water, shook herself off, and Honker stared curiously at the creature in his yard. This visitor looked similar in coloring to him, but it was not similar in size or shape. He turned to Willy and said, "What is this creature?"

Before Willy could answer, the creature started an odd dance and made staccato clucking sounds.

All cats took a stand, fur puffed, tails up, ready for an attack. There was hissing by all four legged animals and suddenly a high-pitched scream came from the new arrival and then Kari, Kris, Sheridan, Garrett, and Kaycee were on the scene.

"Where did this ferret come from?" Kari asked.

"It's a Siamese ferret," Garrett said. "I bet it's somebody's pet."

Little Honker's Backyard Adventure

"I think you're right, but how did it get in the yard?" Kris asked.

"They can burrow under and into lots of things," Sheridan said. "Is there a place around the fence where it could get under or through?"

"I bet there is a place by the garden," Kris said.

"The dirt is loose and it would be easy to get under the fence," Kari said.

"But, if it's somebody's pet, where do you think it came from? How do we find out?" Garrett asked

"You guys know the neighbors around here," Kaycee said. "Is there a family who owns a ferret?"

"Not that I know," Kris said. "But, I bet a little guy like that could slip out pretty easily from most any place. Who knows where it belongs."

The ferret and cats were engaged in a stare-down. Who was the ruler in this situation? The new visitor was giving a warning but not attacking. The regulars in the yard were alerted to the warning but seemed to understand an attack was not needed. Who was in control? Would there be a winner and loser in this stand-off? It was four felines to one ferret. Five humans to one ferret.

Ding Dong. "That's the doorbell." Kris said.

Kari said. "I'll go see who it is."

Kari went into the house to answer the front door.

"Hello. My name is Mary. Have you seen a Siamese ferret around here? My little Frankie escaped somehow."

"Come in," Kari said. "I think Frankie is in our backyard. He's having a bit of a stand-off with the cats."

"You have cats? How many?" Mary asked.

"Well, our new neighbors have three and the only one of our cats outside now is Little Honker, also known as Warren," Kari said. "Follow me."

"I've been so worried," Mary said. "That little guy is such an escape artist and is always getting into something or out of something. We just moved in around the corner. I think our backyards are connected."

The girls walked out of the patio door and into the backyard.

"Hey everybody. This is Mary and the ferret's name is Frankie. I guess he lives in the house behind us," Kari said.

"Welcome to the neighborhood," Kris said.

"Hi," Garrett said. "We just moved in too. These are my sisters Sheridan and Kaycee."

"Happy to meet you guys," Mary said. "I was hoping there would be kids close to my age when we moved here. Frankie, come here."

Mary walked over to Frankie, picked him up, and said, "You are such an escape artist. I should have called you Houdini instead of Frankenstein."

"Why did you call him Frankenstein?" Kaycee asked.

"Because it seemed like he was always trying to create something new in the house. He's a bit of an inventor," she said. "And, sometimes I think he's a little bit of a monster. I love him but he is always creating situations that surprise me," Mary said.

"Well, it looks like Frankie and Honker will be a good team. Honker is always up for something new," Kari said.

"Two Siamese creatures seeking something new? Hold on neighborhood! You all might be in for a big surprise," Kris said.

"I agree," Kaycee said as she leaned down to pick up Fanta.

Mary was still holding Frankie as Kris reached over to pick up Little Honker. "What do you think, Honker? Are our new neighbors going to provide more new adventures for us?"

Little Honker was focused on Fanta and Frankie. The trio's eyes were locked. There seemed to be instant bonding and before Mary, Kaycee, or Kris knew it, the four-legged gang jumped from their humans' arms and were off together.

"There goes the Trio of Trouble!" Garret and Sheridan said at once.

Acknowledgments

First and foremost, I want to thank my husband, Warren, who always reads every draft of every book I have written. He is the one who continues to come up with ideas for perfect endings. I also appreciate all of my other draft readers: Marinell, Doris, Kris, Staci, Shirley, and Margie. They were able to spot everything from typos to needed transition changes.

Another huge thank you to my friend Ruthann Kaiser Rivers who helped me find Sprite, Fanta, and Willy after we lost our dear little Gabby.

A huge thank you to Jenn Porter-Milne for running FUR the Love of Paws FURcility in North Platte, Nebraska, where we were able to adopt our new feline family. Her dedication and love of animals is an inspiration to all! Our new trio provided me with entertainment and adventures that I was able to use in the story. This was especially true with Fanta, the lover of water!

A special thank you to my grandchildren Garrett and Kaycee who read and gave me necessary "kid feedback!" It is always important to test drive and know your audience.

As always I am appreciative of all of the tech support from my dear friend, Lauren, and the Bublish team for assisting me along the way to publication.

About the Author

When Virginia's Siamese cat gave birth to six kittens on her bed, her appreciation for differences and the love of cats started. Cats and students have been a big part of her life for nearly fifty years. Creative Writing was among the high school English courses she taught over her forty years in the classroom. Writing with her students provided her with knowledge of the assignment and led her down the path of discovery. After retirement she was able to follow her passion of writing for young readers. She enjoys reading her books in elementary school classrooms and talking to her audience. In addition to her Little Honker series, she has started to write other animal stories for children. She lives in Colorado with her husband and currently has three rescue cats. She also enjoys being an active grandmother.

www.ingramcontent.com/pod-product-compliance
Lightning Source LLC
Chambersburg PA
CBHW030457010526
44118CB00011B/979